DITCH *the* CAREER

ANDY COATS

AUTHOR

ANDY COATS is an author, artist, adventurer, explorer, and entrepreneur. He loves to tell stories, inspire leaders, and entertain audiences. Since childhood, he has been fascinated by all things adventure and outdoors.

While he has several degrees and even taught collegiate business courses as a professor, he believes the future of business will look different from the traditional model of "get a degree and get a career." He has a passion for inspiring entrepreneurs to take control of their future.

EDITOR

SHANA OVERTON is married to her high school sweetheart, Jake, and homeschools their three little girls. She is a graduate of LSU in Shreveport and obtained her bachelor's degree in Business

Marketing. Shana was a contestant on the Dallas Morning News Spelling Bee and enjoys being teased by friends as a spelling nerd and the grammar police. Her passions are traveling, baking, taking care of her fur baby and chickens, watching her girls do gymnastics, and spending time with family and friends.

ACKNOWLEDGEMENTS

Special Thanks To:

My wonderful wife, Cristi. Thank you for believing in me, supporting me, and pushing me to pursue my dreams.
Love you, babe!

My editor, Shana Overton. Thanks for the recommendations and editing skills. You and Jake are a power couple! We love you guys!

My students over the years. You inspired me to write this book. Chase your dreams and never give up.

My weekly breakfast club– Jess, Stephen, and Bear. Thanks for your listening ears, your encouraging support, and your consistent loyalty.

TABLE OF CONTENTS

Introduction
The Career Trap
>Are You Chained to a Desk or Soaring Towards Your Dreams?

Part 1: Unmasking the Myths
Chapter 1– The 9-to-5 Delusion:
>Office Hours Aren't the Path to Success

Chapter 2– Degrees of Deception:
>Do You Really Need a College Education?

Chapter 3– Corporate Cliffs:
>The Dark Side of Climbing the Ladder

Part 2: Navigating the New Reality
Chapter 4– Freelancing:
>Myths and Rewards

Chapter 5– Digital Nomads:
>Living the Dream Life on Your Terms

Chapter 6– Pursuing Your Passion:
>Turning Your Hobby into a Career

Part 3: Your Path to Potential
Chapter 7– Fear of Failure:
>Overcoming Psychological Barriers to Success

Chapter 8– The Power of Networking:
>Building Your Professional Circle

Chapter 9– Money Matters:
>Financial Freedom and Streams of Income

Conclusion
Reclaiming Your Future:
>Your Guide to Ditching the Career

INTRODUCTION

THE CAREER TRAP

Are You Chained to a Desk or Soaring Towards Your Dreams?

INTRODUCTION

THE CAREER TRAP
Are You Chained to a Desk or Soaring Towards Your Dreams?

Imagine for a moment, the stark contrast between two individuals on a sunny morning. One finds themselves chained to a desk, a heavy weight of routine and obligation pressing down on their shoulders. Their day unfolds predictably, from the oppressive rush hour traffic to the sterile hum of the office. Hours drag on as they dutifully punch keys and count the minutes until they can escape the fluorescent-lit prison, only to repeat the cycle the next day. This is the image of a life constrained, where each minute is a link in an unbreakable chain, and where soaring, it seems, is a distant dream.

Now, let's turn our gaze to another individual on that same morning. They stand on the edge of a cliff, the cool breeze of possibility tousling their hair, overlooking a breathtaking horizon. Their path isn't confined to cubicles and commutes but stretches far beyond the confines of traditional expectations. Their life is a symphony of adventure, exploration, and purpose. With every decision they make, they're charting a course through uncharted territories. Each day brings fresh opportunities and the exhilarating feeling of freedom to explore their own potential. This is the image of a life unchained, where the sky's the limit, and soaring is not only possible but the very essence of existence. Welcome to "Ditch the Career," where we'll show you how to break free from the chains and embrace the limitless sky.

In a world where the conventional path of a steady career seems almost like a rite of passage, it's easy to become entrapped in the narrative that a 9-to-5 job is the only road to success. However, I'm here to tell you that it's time to challenge this age-old script, to shatter the myths that have kept countless individuals confined to their office desks, and to unlock the incredible potential that each of us carries within.

The Career Trap has lured many into a false sense of security. It's the well-trodden path where society tells us that success is measured by climbing a corporate ladder, earning degrees and titles, and adhering to the standard 9-to-5 workday. But what if there's more to life than being chained to a desk and adhering to office hours? In the pages ahead, we'll dissect this conventional narrative, challenging the preconceived notions that have held so many of us back. We'll dare to question whether this path truly leads to happiness and achievement.

The myths we'll uncover in this journey extend beyond the 9-to-5 Delusion. They stretch to the realm of formal education and the notion that a college degree is the sole gateway to success. We'll also delve into the hidden costs and sacrifices of scaling the Corporate Cliffs. It's time to unveil the truths that have been obscured by the allure of steady employment.

We'll scrutinize these myths from every angle, empowering you with the knowledge needed to make informed decisions about your future.

Are you ready to navigate the New Reality? In Part 2, we'll expose the fallacies surrounding freelancing and explore the world of digital nomads—individuals who've shattered the traditional work mold to embrace lifestyles filled with adventure, freedom, and unique opportunities. We'll challenge the stereotypes and doubts that often surround those who dare to turn their passions into their paycheck. This section is all about understanding the alternative paths available and equipping you with the knowledge and insights to decide whether they align with your aspirations.

Now, imagine living a life where you're not a cog in the corporate machine but a creator of your own destiny. It's not just a dream; it's a new reality for many. As we journey together through these pages, we'll reveal the powerful tools for navigating this new landscape, the psychology of overcoming fear of failure, and the art of building a network that can transform your life. Whether you seek financial freedom, work-life balance, or a sense of purpose, you'll find the inspiration and guidance needed to uncover your unique potential. In this book, you will boldly explore how the traditional concept of a career can be misleading and confining and examine how to embrace alternative routes to personal and professional fulfillment. Your path to potential begins here.

PART 1

UNMASKING THE MYTHS

The 9-to-5 Delusion

Degrees of Deception

Corporate Cliffs

CHAPTER 1

THE 9-to-5 DELUSION

Office Hours Aren't the Path to Success

CHAPTER 1

THE 9-to-5 DELUSION
Office Hours Aren't the Path to Success

Welcome to the realm of the 9-to-5 delusion, where the daily grind feels less like a routine and more like a rerun of a rather uninspiring sitcom. It's a world where waking up at the crack of dawn, navigating rush-hour traffic, and slogging through mind-numbing meetings are as inevitable as death and taxes. So, let's put on our comedic glasses and take a closer look at this charade.

As the sun rises, the 9-to-5 warriors embark on their epic quest, armed with briefcases and steaming cups of liquid sanity. The workplace beckons with fluorescent lights so bright they could double as tanning beds, and the aroma of instant coffee that may pass as jet fuel. If you're lucky, the office plant survived the night since you've forgotten to water it for the past three weeks.

Now, here's a quote to ponder as we dissect this delusion: "The 9-to-5 may be a joke, but no one's laughing." It's high time we asked ourselves whether productivity should be measured by the sheer number of hours spent chained to the desk. After all, even a broken clock is right twice a day. So why should your most innovative ideas be confined to those prescribed office hours?

"Success isn't about how early you rise, but how high you soar."

Let's break the shackles of this chronologically obsessed culture and embrace the flexible, tech-powered world that's right at our fingertips. Your office could be a cozy cafe with free Wi-Fi and endless lattes. If you've ever felt a surge of creativity while sipping your double mocha latte, you know the truth.

And don't let the delusion fool you into thinking that sacrificing personal time and relationships is a badge of honor. Remember, "Success at work shouldn't come at the cost of a life well-lived." In fact, many of history's greatest minds had their "aha" moments in the most unconventional places and times – the shower, during a midnight snack, or while waiting for the microwave to ding.

Now, imagine a world where your workday aligns with your natural rhythm. Your "Monday morning" could be your "Wednesday night" if that's when you're firing on all cylinders. The 9-to-5 delusion overlooks the individuality of people and their peak hours, as if the entire human race could synchronize their creativity like a choreographed dance.

So, as we journey through this chapter, let's do so with a chuckle and the wisdom that the 9-to-5 delusion isn't just a comedy sketch; it's a cautionary tale. It's time to tear down the cubicle walls, uncuff yourself from your desk, and embrace a world of opportunities that better suit your unique aspirations and energy. It's a brave new world out there, and you're ready to seize it with humor and ambition.

If you've made it this far, then you're probably interested in learning how to escape this death cycle. You're probably tired of the nausea that happens on Sunday nights as you think about Monday morning, bothered by how many times you reference Wednesday being Hump Day, and sick of the emotional roller coaster that happens when you realize Thursday isn't Friday. If this is you, know that you are not alone. I'm here to help you escape the prison.

Let's Look at FIVE Reasons Why Office Hours aren't the Pathway to Success:

1. Creativity Doesn't Punch a Clock

Let's face it, creativity doesn't wear a wristwatch. It's not sitting in a tiny office cubicle, diligently waiting for that 9 AM start time, sipping its coffee, and saying, "Okay, folks, time to innovate!" No, creativity is more like that spontaneous friend who calls you at 2 AM and says, "Hey, I've got this brilliant idea!" The 9-to-

5 routine is like telling your genius friend to come back between 9 and 5 if they want to be heard. Sorry, but the universe doesn't work on an office clock. If it did, we'd have had Einstein's Theory of Relativity delivered during a Monday morning meeting.

2. Quality Trumps Quantity

It's not about the hours, it's about the brainpower. Picture this: you've been staring at your computer screen for hours, contemplating the profound mysteries of your stapler. You've attended back-to-back meetings that could rival a seminar on "Advanced Origami Paper Folding." In the 9-to-5 world, it's like they're judging success by the thickness of your chair's indentation. Let's be honest, it's not about how long you sit; it's about what you do while you're there. We could all be "busy" for eight hours straight, but is your "busy" producing results, or are you just adding another email to your inbox? Remember, it's not about the quantity; it's about the quality, and no one ever won a marathon by sprinting in circles.

3. Chasing Happiness on the Weekends

"Living for the weekend" is a cry for help. So, you're working your tail off from Monday to Friday, just to get to the weekend? It's like saying, "I'll endure five days of microwave meals and bad coffee to savor two days of Netflix binges and weekend warrior adventures." If your definition of success means enduring most of your life to enjoy a sliver of it, you might want to reconsider. Life is happening right now, not just on Saturdays and Sundays. Success should be measured by how much you love every day of the week, not just the two you've circled on your calendar. Besides, those weekend dance moves could use some weekday practice!

4. Ignoring Individual Rhythms

In the 9-to-5 world, night owls are considered aliens and everyone's expected to be a chipper morning person. What about those nocturnal creatures who get their best work done when the rest of the world is peacefully snoring? In the 9-to-5 realm, they're treated like UFO sightings, a rare and misunderstood breed. "You work best at 2 AM? You must be an alien!" It's as if society says, "Hey, your biological clock is in the wrong time zone, pal!" Success isn't a matter of which hours you keep; it's what you do with those hours. So, if you're most productive during the hours when the bats are on their coffee break, more power to you!

5. AI: The Robot Rebellion... of the Mundane

Let's not forget our impending robot overlords! Yes, AI is here, and it's got its greedy electronic eyes set on those mundane, soul-sucking tasks that we love to hate. You know, the "can you please update these spreadsheets" or the "let's organize this endless stack of papers" kind of jobs. If there was ever a revolution, it would be the rebellion of the bored, paper-shuffling robots! It's like the office photocopier whispering to your desk, "Soon, my friend, we shall be free from this drudgery!" So, in this brave new world, why stick to the 9-to-5 when your AI coworker is thrilled to take over the most mundane parts of your job? It's a win-win; you get more interesting work, and your robot buddy gets to digitize the thousandth memo of the day! Success is making friends in high-tech places. While there is much to be said about artificial intelligence, I want to point out that it's unnecessary for you to do the mundane when AI can do it for you.

As you reflect on these insights, ask yourself: Are you nurturing your creativity beyond the confines of a schedule? Are your efforts focused on quality rather than mere quantity? Is success a daily pursuit, or are you merely living for the weekends? Do you honor your individual rhythms, and are you ready to embrace the technological shifts that redefine the workplace?

In the end, the hope lies in the realization that success is a dynamic, personal journey. It's about breaking free from the constraints of tradition, celebrating diversity, and adapting to the evolving landscape.

The canvas is yours to paint, and the masterpiece awaits your unique brushstroke.

So, how will you shape your success in this ever-changing world?

What steps will you take to infuse passion and purpose into each moment?

REFLECTION

____

____

____

____

____

____

____

____

CHAPTER 2

DEGREES OF DECEPTION

Do You Really Need a College Education?

CHAPTER 2

DEGREES OF DECEPTION
Do You Really Need a College Education?

Ah, college! The time-honored tradition of young adults paying exorbitant sums to acquire knowledge they could find for free on the internet. Yes, it's a common rite of passage that many embark upon, but as with any great adventure, it has its fair share of pitfalls. So, let's delve into the world of higher education, where you'll find not everything is scholarly serenity.

I want to give you a little background about me. Due to my academic pursuits, I racked up an abundance of student loan debt. Now, I learned a great deal about business, leadership, religion, and education while in undergraduate and graduate school; however, most of my practical education came from my life experience—and from watching videos on the Internet. It's not that I don't value education, but I have seen the unnecessary waste and expense that happens in higher education for the average student.

I'm a former college professor who taught business education in college. It was there that I realized students were hungry for practical, life-changing knowledge and experience—not concepts and philosophies only. It was then that I shifted my teaching to incorporate practical, real-world insights. So, I'm not just throwing stones from the outside—I'm throwing them from the inside as well.

The Pros and Cons of College

Now, before we dive into the delightful drawbacks, let's give credit where credit is due. College, that hallowed institution, can be a magical place. During freshman year in college, I was on a National Championship Powerlifting team. It was one of the most incredible experiences of my life. I also met my wife in graduate school and I'm grateful that she's in my life. The hardest part about graduate school was managing my desire to spend time with her while also writing a fair amount of papers and reading books!

College is where I learned the art of procrastination to an Olympic level. I was the world's best at writing a 10-page paper the night before it was due and submitting assignments at 11:58pm. I also discovered the finest ways to survive on a diet of instant noodles, cold pizza, and energy drinks. Plus, I even mastered the skill of sleeping through a class and waking myself up with my own snoring. Oh, and education! Of course, I got an education along the way.

Certainly, while college can be essential for many, especially those pursuing careers in highly specialized fields such as medicine, engineering, or academia, it may not be the ideal route for the entrepreneurs and creatives diving into this book. For those who thrive on innovation, creativity, and the entrepreneurial spirit, the rigid structure of college can sometimes feel like a square peg in a round hole.

You're likely an individual with a zest for forging your own path, unencumbered by traditional academic structures. You're probably more drawn to learning by doing, seeking opportunities outside the classroom, and carving your own unique journey to success. College, for you, might not be the ideal launchpad for your innovative ideas and ventures, and this book aims to provide you with alternative strategies to flourish in the ever-evolving landscape of the creative and entrepreneurial world.

While college can be great, it's not all sunshine and Shakespearean soliloquies. The reality is, college can be the fast lane to a student loan debt nightmare. Picture yourself in a fiery chariot of loan repayments, being chased by a pack of irate loan officers with pitchforks. It's a daunting reality when you graduate, and your degree certificate gleams while your bank account screams.

However, we now live in the Information Age. The world has changed, my friends. We now exist in the era of instant information gratification. Anything you want to learn, you can find online, often for free. That's right, folks, the internet isn't just for memes and cat videos; it's a treasure trove of knowledge. So, why pay through the nose for textbooks and lectures when you can learn almost anything from the comfort of your pajamas?

Here are **FOUR** Reasons to Reconsider the College Conundrum:

1. Financial Freedom:

You know what's liberating? Not being shackled to student loan debt for the next few decades. By skipping the college route, you'll be lightyears ahead in terms of financial freedom. Instead of funneling money into tuition, you can start saving, investing, and pursuing your passions.

2. Time is Money (and Opportunities):

While your peers are sitting in lectures, you could be gaining real-world experience. It's the classic trade-off – college requires years, whereas the real world offers opportunities to learn, grow, and, dare we say, earn. And those years can add up to a lot of experience and a potential head start in your career.

3. Creativity Unleashed:

College can sometimes be the creativity crusher. The rigid structure and conventional curriculum may stifle your innovative spirit. Skipping college opens up the possibility to dive headfirst into your creative endeavors or entrepreneurial dreams without the academic handcuffs.

4. Learning by Doing:

The best way to learn something is by doing it. Instead of memorizing endless facts, you can gain hands-on experience and practical skills in your chosen field. It's like learning to swim by jumping into the pool rather than reading a book about swimming.

So, as we navigate the college conundrum, remember that a degree might not be the golden ticket it once was. While college has its perks, it's not a one-size-fits-all solution. In this wacky, wonderful world, you have options, and a degree isn't the only path to success. Just think of it as one big choose-your-own-adventure novel with a few humorously, perilous twists and turns.

REFLECTION

____

____

____

____

____

____

____

____

CHAPTER 3

CORPORATE CLIFFS

The Dark Side of Climbing the Ladder

CHAPTER 3

CORPORATE CLIFFS
The Dark Side of Climbing the Ladder

My wife, Cristi, and I love to climb mountains. We have reached more than 20 summits of mountains over 14,000' in elevation. In my mountaineering experience, one of the things I've realized is that climbing is all about risk assessment. Before every climb, we evaluate the risk versus the reward. In a corporate setting, climbing the career ladder comes with significant risks.

Corporate America, despite its polished look and towering office buildings, is one of the riskiest occupational paths you can take. Oftentimes, it feels like a high-stakes poker game for careers—where every move can be as uncertain as trying to predict the weather in March. Job security is like chasing Bigfoot—you want to believe it's out there, but it has an uncanny ability to disappear just when you thought you had a grip on it.

The relentless pressure to meet performance targets can turn the most optimistic, confident professionals into fearful employees that tread lightly and fearfully, like tourists walking across a glass-bottom bridge. With corporate restructuring announcements happening so frequently, it's a world where career trajectories feel unpredictable. Thus, every step up the corporate ladder becomes a thrilling gamble in the grand casino of professional achievement.

Ah, the corporate ladder, a treacherous ascent, often pursued with fervor and single-minded determination. For many, the pursuit of corporate success becomes an all-encompassing mission that often feels similar to rolling a boulder up a hill only to have it tumble

back down on you. As we've cheerfully explored
explored the lighter side of corporate life, it's
only fitting to acknowledge the shadowy under-
belly that awaits those who put all their career
eggs in this basket. So, buckle up and put on
your safety helmet; we're about to explore how
climbing the corporate ladder can be a risky
endeavor.

Here are TEN Corporate Cliffs and the Risks Associated with Them:

1. Job Insecurity:

The corporate world is notorious for its
shifting sands, and job security is often akin
to trying to build a sandcastle as the tide rolls
in – precarious at best. Loyalty to a company
can be shattered in an instant due to mergers,
downsizing, or changes in market conditions.
The looming threat of job loss keeps employees
on edge, and this constant uncertainty can take
a toll on mental health and financial stability. It's
like standing on a melting iceberg, never quite
sure when it will give way.

2. Burnout:

The relentless pursuit of corporate success can lead to mental and physical exhaustion, resulting in burnout that can impact not only your career, but also your overall well-being. The never-ending demands of the corporate world can push you to the brink, making it feel as if you're running a marathon without a finish line. Burnout affects not only your job performance, but can also seep into your personal life, causing strain on relationships and a sense of persistent fatigue that's hard to shake.

3. Stress:

The pressure to meet performance metrics can transform the workplace into a pressure cooker, where stress levels can reach astronomical heights. The constant scrutiny, the fear of falling short, and the drive to outperform your peers can lead to chronic stress. It's like carrying an ever-increasing weight on your shoulders, and the cumulative stress can take a toll on your mental health, causing anxiety, depression, and other related issues.

4. Office Politics:

Navigating the treacherous waters of office politics can feel like trying to sail through a minefield without a map. The need to build alliances and protect your position can lead to a web of intrigue and deception. The constant need to decipher others' motives and play the game can be emotionally exhausting, creating a toxic work environment where trust is often in short supply. It's like living in a constant state of political intrigue, where the wrong move can spell disaster for your career.

5. Work-Life Imbalance:

The all-encompassing nature of corporate life can disrupt your work-life balance, leaving you feeling like a juggler trying to keep multiple balls in the air. Long hours, demanding deadlines, and the pressure to be constantly available can make it challenging to dedicate time to personal life, hobbies, and relaxation. This imbalance can lead to strained relationships, a lack of personal fulfillment, and a sense of being constantly stretched to the limit.

6. Eroding Health:

The sedentary nature of many office jobs and the pursuit of success can lead to a decline in physical health, as if you're trading in vitality for a higher rung on the ladder. Spending prolonged hours at a desk, coupled with the stress of the corporate world, can result in unhealthy lifestyle choices, including poor diet and lack of exercise. The toll on your health can lead to weight gain, increased risk of chronic illnesses, and a decreased overall quality of life.

7. The Illusion of Success:

Climbing the corporate ladder can lead to a hollow victory when you reach the top and discover that the view isn't as grand as expected. Success, as defined by corporate standards, can often feel empty, with the pursuit of titles and paychecks overshadowing personal fulfillment and happiness. It's like scaling a mountain only to find that the summit isn't as breathtaking as you imagined.

8. Layoffs and Restructuring:

The corporate world is filled with restructurings, mergers, and layoffs, making job security as elusive as the horizon. The threat of losing your job due to factors beyond your control can be a constant source of anxiety. It's like walking a tightrope, never quite sure when it might snap, leading to financial instability and emotional distress.

9. Narrow Focus:

A single-minded pursuit of corporate success can lead to tunnel vision, causing you to miss out on alternative paths to personal and professional growth. The intense focus on climbing the corporate ladder can narrow your perspective, limiting your exploration of other interests, skills, and opportunities. It's like wearing blinders that prevent you from seeing the broader landscape of potential avenues for success and fulfillment.

10. Lost Perspective:

With the constant drive to ascend, it's easy to lose sight of what truly matters in life – relationships, personal growth, and the simple joys that bring happiness beyond corporate achievements. The relentless pursuit of corporate success can lead to neglect of family, friends, and self-care. It's like being on a fast-moving train that doesn't allow time for the appreciation of life's small, precious moments. It's vital to remember that true success encompasses a balanced, fulfilling life that extends beyond the corporate realm.

Have I made you regret your decision to be in Corporate America?

The reality is that if you're reading this and you're in Corporate America, then you know this all too well. However, if you need further convincing, let me conclude by saying how brutal and toxic it can be. Don't waste your best years climbing the corporate ladder only to realize it doesn't lead where you want to be. So, it's essential to reflect on the insights gained from this chapter and their real-world application to help provide a solution. I have unveiled the harsh realities often concealed behind the traditional corporate ladder, emphasizing that success shouldn't be defined solely by the number of rungs we ascend. There are alternative routes to professional fulfillment and purpose.

The key takeaway here is to reevaluate your career ambitions, recognizing that success can be achieved through lateral moves, entrepreneurial ventures, or by crafting your unique path. As you move forward, consider your own values, well-being, and the larger impact you wish to make. The corporate ladder isn't the only route to success; it's one of many, and the choice is yours.

REFLECTION

____

____

____

____

____

____

Go to...
N
NW
NE
W
E
SW
SE
S
0
20
45
60
80
100
120
140
160
180
200
220
240
260
280
300
320
340

PART 2

NAVIGATING THE
NEW REALITY

Freelancing

Digital Nomads

Pursuing Your Passion

CHAPTER 4

FREELANCING

Myths and Rewards

CHAPTER 4

FREELANCING
Myths and Rewards

In the realm of the workforce, freelancers are the brave individuals who have chosen the path of self-employment. Imagine a world where the traditional office is replaced by your favorite cozy café, the monotonous commute is a leisurely stroll to your favorite spot in the park, and the strict 9-to-5 schedule gives way to the flexible rhythm of your choosing. This is the inspiring dream of freelancing, where you are not just an employee, but the master of your own professional universe.

Picture a life where you decide the projects you take on, set your own working hours, and even design your workspace to reflect your unique style and preferences. It's a world where your skills and passions are the compass guiding your career, and the possibilities are as vast as your imagination.

In this world of freelance freedom, you become a storyteller, designer, programmer, consultant, or whatever your heart desires. Your laptop is your bridge to a global marketplace, where you can collaborate with clients from different corners of the world. The thrill of diverse projects keeps every day fresh and exciting, as you explore various industries, cultures, and challenges. More than just work, freelancing is a lifestyle. It's about discovering the beauty of balancing your professional and personal life, and the joy of being present for life's precious moments.

Freelancing is a lifestyle

Your journey as a freelancer is not only about financial success; but it's also about the freedom to sculpt your destiny, to chase your passions, and to create your unique definition of prosperity. So, if you're yearning for a life where you can say goodbye to cubicles and hello to boundless horizons, the path to freelance freedom is paved with golden opportunities.

Maybe that inspired you to take the leap. But for many of you, you just felt a rush of fear and anxiety. Why? Probably because you have heard war stories of failed ventures and unsuccessful attempts for freedom. I want to help ease some of the emotion. Amidst the tales of the freelancing professional journey, there exists both misconceptions and genuine benefits. So, let's take a look at both.

Myth 1: The Myth of Being Lazy and Sloppy

The myth that freelancers work in their pajamas is far from the truth. While it's true that you can work in comfortable attire, freelancers must maintain a professional image, especially during client interactions. Freelancing requires self-discipline and systematic planning. Laziness and messiness aren't a byproduct of being a freelancer; however, freelancing can highlight those character flaws.

Myth 2: The Myth of Casually Hanging Out in Coffee Shops

The coffee shop, often portrayed as the freelancer's haven, is a double-edged sword. While it provides a change of scenery, it can also be a challenging place to work due to limited access to power outlets and less-than-ideal Wi-Fi speeds. However, oftentimes freelancers spend a lot of time in cafes—giving them a neutral, consistent place for meeting with clients and getting work done without having to pay for expensive office space.

Myth 3: The Myth of Eternal Vacation

Freelancers don't have an everlasting vacation. Their envious schedules can seem flexible to a confined employee who is imprisoned to the 9-5 schedule. However, their job can be demanding, with long hours and the need to meet project deadlines. Sometimes, flexibility can appear to be freedom from responsibility. This can cause the traditional employee to be jealous of those with flexibility and freedom.

Myth 4: Freelancing is a Get-Rich-Quick Scheme

Freelancing is not a guaranteed path to quick wealth. Freelancers work hard to earn their income, often managing multiple clients and facing budget constraints. Usually, free-lancers spend the first several years just trying to break even. Sometimes, flexibility can appear to be freedom from responsibility.

Myth 5: All Fun and No Responsibility

Freelancers have a significant degree of autonomy, but they also have responsibilities. Managing their own business and juggling var-ious clients can be complex and demanding. Oftentimes, they are juggling many tasks and wearing many business hats.

Here are FIVE Benefits of Freelancing:

1. Flexibility

Freelancers have the freedom to set their own work hours, providing flexibility to accommodate personal commitments. Having a flexible schedule affords them the ability to have extended lunches, go to their kids' activities, and possibly work from anywhere at any time.

2. Diverse Projects

Freelancers often have the opportunity to work on a wide range of projects, which keeps their work engaging and diverse. Freelancers typically like variety and change, so having this diversity is like a dream come true. It prevents burnout and eliminates the mundane.

3. No Commute

Eliminating the daily commute is a significant benefit, saving time and reducing stress related to traffic. This time savings can help reduce costs, increase location flexibility, and give freelancers several hours per week that can be devoted to working instead of commuting.

4. Autonomy

Freelancers have control over their work,

making decisions independently without the need to answer to a superior.

5. Passion Pursuit

Freelancing allows individuals to pursue projects that align with their interests and passions, enabling them to find fulfillment in their work.

Freelancing presents misconceptions, but it also offers genuine rewards. It's a realm where autonomy and diverse projects can provide significant benefits. However, it's important to recognize the challenges and responsibilities that come with the territory. For those who choose to explore the world of freelancing, it offers a unique and fulfilling professional journey.

REFLECTION

____

____

____

____

____

CHAPTER 5

DIGITAL NOMADS

Living the Dream Life on
Your Terms

CHAPTER 5

DIGITAL NOMADS
Living the Dream Life on
Your Terms

Imagine a life where your office is a beach in Bali, a cozy cafe in Paris, or a mountain cabin in the Swiss Alps. Welcome to the world of digital nomads, a community of modern-day adventurers who've cracked the code to work on their own terms. Digital nomads enjoy the freedom to explore new cultures, experience different cuisines, and make friends all over the world while still earning a substantial income.

As we delve into this exciting world, remember that with the right blend of ambition, skills, and adaptability, you can be the captain of your ship, steering it toward the most enticing destinations, and living the dream life on your own terms. In this chapter, we'll dive into the inspiring realm of digital nomadism and explore remarkable businesses where individuals can work remotely from any corner of the globe while making six-figure incomes or more, all while maintaining the coveted freedoms of flexible schedules and minimal hours.

Here are SEVEN Remote Businesses that can earn Six-Figures:

1. Freelance Writing and Content Creation

- Content creators can write articles, blog posts, or marketing materials for clients in various industries.
- Six-figure income potential can come from establishing a solid client base, securing high-paying projects, and continuously improving writing skills.
- Flexible work hours allow writers to tailor their schedules around travel, exploration, and personal pursuits.
- Minimal hours can be achieved by efficiently managing projects and enhancing productivity.

2. Dropshipping and E-Commerce

- Digital nomads can create e-commerce stores and partner with suppliers who handle inventory and shipping.
- Success in dropshipping depends on selecting profitable niches, marketing effectively, and managing customer service.
- The flexibility of e-commerce allows nomads to travel and manage their business remotely.
- Once the initial setup is complete, the time required to run a dropshipping store can be minimal, especially when automated processes are in place.

3. Online Coaching and Consulting

- Coaches and consultants can offer services in areas like life coaching, business strategy, health and wellness, and more.
- Six-figure incomes are attainable through building a strong reputation, securing high-paying clients, and offering valuable expertise.
- Flexibility is inherent, as sessions can be conducted via video calls from anywhere in the world.

- Minimal hours can be achieved by structuring your consulting or coaching practice to your liking, whether through fewer clients or optimized session schedules.

4. Affiliate Marketing

- Affiliate marketers promote products or services from other companies and earn a commission on sales.
- Success comes from selecting profitable affiliate programs, building an online presence, and generating sales.
- The flexibility of affiliate marketing allows digital nomads to manage their marketing efforts from any location.
- Minimal hours can be achieved by setting up passive income streams through well-optimized content and marketing strategies.

5. Remote Software Development

- Software developers and programmers can work on various projects remotely, from app development to web development.
- Six-figure incomes are common in this field,

with demand for skilled developers constantly growing.
- Software developers have the ability to work from anywhere in the world.
- Minimal hours can be challenging, as project deadlines can vary, but efficient coding and project management can help streamline work.

6. Online Courses and E-Learning

- Creating and selling online courses on platforms like Udemy or your own website can be a lucrative business.
- Income potential is high, especially if courses gain popularity and receive positive reviews.
- The flexibility to manage courses from anywhere allows digital nomads to teach while traveling.
- Minimal hours can be achieved by creating courses as an initial effort, and then periodically updating or maintaining them.

7. Virtual Administrative Services

- Virtual assistants offer administrative support to businesses, from email management to

scheduling and bookkeeping.
- Building a client base and offering specialized services can lead to a six-figure income.
- Digital nomads have the flexibility to choose clients and work on a wide array of tasks from their location.
- Minimal hours can be achieved by efficient task management, outsourcing, and working with several clients to reduce reliance on a single source of income.

These digital nomad business options offer diverse opportunities for individuals seeking freedom, flexibility, and the potential for significant income while exploring the world. Success in each of these areas requires dedication, skill development, and a strong work ethic, but the rewards are well worth the effort for those who value a nomadic lifestyle and professional independence. The digital nomad lifestyle is not just a dream; it's an achievable reality.

In the dynamic realm of remote work as a digital nomad, self-discipline and efficient systems are the cornerstones of success. The absence of a traditional office structure demands a heightened level of personal responsibility and accountability. Self-discipline becomes the driving force behind meeting deadlines, staying focused amidst potential distractions, and maintaining a healthy work-life balance.

Without the structure imposed by a physical workspace, the digital nomad must cultivate a strong internal framework to navigate the vast and often uncharted waters of remote work. A disciplined approach ensures that tasks are completed efficiently and consistently, fostering a sense of accomplishment and professionalism.

Equally vital is the establishment of robust systems to streamline workflows. Digital nomads often find themselves juggling multiple tasks, collaborating with team members across different time zones, and adapting to ever-changing environments. Implementing effective systems for communication, project management, and task organization not only enhances productivity but also provides a sense of stability in an otherwise fluid work setting.

A well-designed system acts as a compass, guiding the digital nomad through the complexities of remote work and enabling them to navigate challenges with ease. As the digital landscape continues to evolve, the ability to cultivate self-discipline and implement efficient systems becomes increasingly crucial for those seeking success in the realm of remote work.

How can you strengthen your self-discipline to consistently meet your work goals as a digital nomad?

____

____

____

____

What systems and tools have proven most effective for optimizing your remote work experience, and how can you adapt them to evolving circumstances?

____

____

____

____

Reflecting on your personal strategies for self-discipline and system implementation can lead to valuable insights that contribute to your ongoing success as a digital nomad.

REFLECTION

CHAPTER 6

PURSUING YOUR PASSION

Turning Your Hobby Into Your Career

CHAPTER 6

PURSUING YOUR PASSION
Turning Your Hobby Into Your Career

In a world where the daily grind is the norm, pursuing your passion and transforming it into a career may sound like a dream too good to be true. Picture a world where your work isn't just a job; instead, you are getting paid large sums of money to do what you love. It's a bit like finding out that unicorns are real, except this dream can actually come true. As you'll discover in this chapter, this dream of yours can indeed become a reality. We'll explore the immeasurable value and benefits of turning your passion into a profession, with the inspirational journey of Elon Musk as a shining example.

The Value of Pursuing Your Passion

When you chase your dreams, it's like adding a sprinkle of fairy dust to your everyday life. Choosing a career aligned with your passion infuses each workday with joy and enthusiasm. When you're motivated by your passion, it's not just a job – it's a fulfilling journey where work doesn't feel like a chore. Work becomes a magical journey where Mondays don't feel like a prison sentence, and Fridays might just be the beginning of another exciting project. Plus, the benefits extend far beyond personal happiness; they often lead to a higher level of performance and creativity.

Choosing a career aligned with your passion infuses each workday with joy and enthusiasm

---

When you're passionate about what you do, you become as unstoppable as a caffeinated squirrel. You'll perform better, innovate like a genius, and bring a level of creativity that rivals the videos of internet influencers.

Elon Musk, the visionary entrepreneur behind SpaceX and Tesla, epitomizes this truth. His unwavering passion for space exploration and clean energy has not only revolutionized these industries, but also rewarded him with immense success. As a nice bonus, pioneering these passion project companies has even rocketed him into the billionaire's club. Not to mention, he's living the dream of launching rockets and electric cars into the cosmos – not your average day job!

Musk's relentless pursuit of space exploration, through SpaceX, aims to make humanity multi-planetary. His passion for electric vehicles and sustainable energy, as seen with Tesla, has ushered in a new era of automotive technology and energy efficiency. His dedication to solving these global challenges aligns perfectly with his passions, and the rewards have been astronomical, both in terms of personal fulfillment and financial success.

To get you started on exploring potential passions you can turn into business opportunities, here are a few options to consider.

Here are **TEN** Hobbies that can become Profitable Small Businesses:

1. Photography

- Start a photography business specializing in portraits, events, or stock photography.
- Develop a portfolio, invest in quality equipment, and market your services.
- Provide photo services for events such as weddings, engagements, graduations, head-shots, anniversaries, gender reveals, seasonal portraits, and youth sports teams.
- Find your niche and master it.

2. Crafting and Handmade Goods

- Turn your love for crafting into a business selling handmade jewelry, candles, or seasonal decorations like ornaments or door wreaths.
- Create an online store, establish your unique style, and engage with potential customers on platforms like Etsy.
- Use social media to develop a community where you engage customers with videos of you making these crafts.

- Host parties where you teach people to make a small craft and then sell your products in person and/or take orders.

3. Cooking and Baking

- Open a catering or bakery business, offering your culinary delights to the public.
- Comply with food safety regulations, create a diverse menu, and build a loyal customer base.
- Start with a simple menu focused around your best items and introduce a seasonal menu to help keep your customers coming back regularly.
- If you get overly booked, hire some friends or fellow cooking enthusiasts to join you. Then, share the proceeds with them.

4. Fitness and Personal Training

- Become a certified personal trainer and provide fitness coaching services.
- Advertise your expertise online, collaborate with local gyms, and offer personalized training programs.

- Host some free outdoor group fitness sessions as introductory opportunities for people to receive further personalized services.
- Put together and offer coaching and nutrition plans for individuals to gain monthly, recurring income.

5. Gardening and Landscaping

- Launch a landscaping or gardening services business, transforming outdoor spaces.
- Build a professional portfolio, invest in quality tools, and market your services in your community.
- Spend a lot of effort on making your yard the best in the neighborhood and then put a small promotional sign out front on the day you cut the grass.
- Start local and offer incentives for referrals that turn into customers (1 month free for 3 successful referrals).

6. Writing and Blogging

- Start a blog, write articles, or self-publish books on topics that resonate with you.

- Create engaging content, build an online following, and explore monetization options like ads, affiliate marketing, or sponsored posts.
- Utilize AI tools to help you when you get writer's block or need a creative nudge.
- One of the best places to start is by creating a small 40-50 page E-Book on a topic you are passionate about.

7. Graphic Design

- Provide graphic design services for businesses or clients looking for logos, branding ideas, and web designs.
- Build a strong portfolio, network with potential clients, and offer competitive pricing.
- Businesses are in need of social media graphics, logo and branding help, and much more.
- Offer a free branding consultation to a business. Show them areas where they need improvement. Offer, for free, some small areas they can fix themselves. Then, for larger branding opportunities with greater returns, offer your services to them with a schedule and pricing.

8. Pet Care and Pet Sitting

- Establish a pet care or pet sitting business, catering to pet owners in need of reliable services.
- Gain relevant certifications, create a website or social media page, and utilize word-of-mouth referrals.
- With the rise in boarding costs, offering quality, personalized services could prove very lucrative.

9. Fishing and Outdoor Adventures

- Outdoor adventure tours and excursions for enthusiasts.
- Obtain necessary permits and licenses, create exciting packages, and market your business online and through tourism agencies.
- Start by planning an outdoor adventure trip for a local school or scout group.
- Offer leadership and/or teamwork elements built into the program.
- Additional adventures could include hunting, hiking, mountain climbing, rafting, kayaking, etc.

10. DIY Home Improvement

- Provide home improvement services such as painting, repairs, or remodeling.
- Acquire essential tools, showcase before-and-after photos, and build a strong local reputation through word of mouth and online reviews.
- Remember, sometimes doing small tasks and projects could be very lucrative. If you do 1,000 small tasks over the entire year for $50 each, then that's an additional $50k per year. Not to mention, the once-per-month big projects you get. This could easily be a six-figure side hustle.

Here are THREE Important Steps to Transforming Your Hobby into a Business:

1. Assessment and Preparation

- Evaluate the demand and competition in your chosen hobby-turned-business.
- Invest in essential equipment or certifications to provide quality services.
- Craft a business plan that outlines your target audience, pricing strategy, and goals.

2. Marketing and Branding

- Establish an online presence through a professional website and/or active social media accounts.
- Showcase your passion and expertise through compelling content and visual representation.
- Network with potential clients and industry peers to build a strong reputation.

3. Scaling and Growth

- Continuously refine your services and seek feedback from clients.
- Expand your business through client referrals, diversified services, and targeted advertising.
- Stay adaptable and open to growth opportunities as your business evolves.

Transforming your passion into a business not only offers personal fulfillment, but also the potential for substantial financial rewards. It's a journey that requires dedication, strategic planning, and unwavering enthusiasm, and when aligned with your true interests, the possibilities are limitless.

So, why not embark on this exciting adventure and turn your hobbies into a thriving career that will help you reach your goals and dreams?

73

REFLECTION

____

____

____

____

____

____

____

PART 3

YOUR PATH TO POTENTIAL

Fear of Failure

The Power of Networking

Money Matters

CHAPTER 7

FEAR OF FAILURE

Overcoming Psychological Barriers to Success

CHAPTER 7

FEAR OF FAILURE
Overcoming Psychological Barriers to Success

The fear of failure can be like a shadow, silently lurking, ready to prevent your every move. It has the power to stop you from pursuing your dreams. But here's the secret: failure is not your enemy; it's a stepping stone on the path to success. In this chapter, we'll explore the paralyzing grip of the fear of failure, the incredible value of using failure as an opportunity to learn and grow, and the five psychological barriers that can hinder your journey to financial independence through self-employment. For each barrier, we'll unveil a definition, a description, and three steps to overcome it.

The Paralyzing Fear of Failure

The fear of failure can feel like quicksand, pulling you into a sinkhole of doubt and uncertainty. It whispers in your ear, making you question your every decision. It's like having a relentless critic living in your head, pointing out all the ways you might stumble, fall, and never recover. But what if I told you that this very fear holds the key to unlocking your potential?

Embracing Failure as a Learning Opportunity

Failure isn't a tombstone marking the end; it's a signpost pointing you toward valuable lessons to be learned along the journey. Each failure is a teacher, and its lessons are the price of admission to the school of success. Failure teaches resilience, innovation, and determination. It's the forge where you become stronger and more resilient. It's not the end; it's a detour on the road to victory.

Overcoming Psychological Barriers

I want to help you work through the obstacles that I know you are going to face; however, please don't replace professional or clinical advice with my recommendations. In my experience, I have seen the power of positive and negative thinking, but I am not an expert in psychological matters. I strongly advise seeking professional guidance for matters where your mental health and well-being are concerned. With that being said, I want to give you a launching pad from a business perspective to help you overcome the psychological barriers you're going to likely face as you seek to take control of your future.

Here are the FIVE Barriers and How to Find Victory

1. FEAR OF JUDGEMENT

Definition:
The fear of judgment is the apprehension of being negatively evaluated by others, which often hinders personal and professional progress.

Description:

The fear of "what will everyone else think?" This fear of judgment can hit close to home, causing concern about how your friends, family, or colleagues might perceive your choices. It might make you hesitate when considering self-employment, as the thought of potential disapproval can overshadow your passions and ideas.

Steps Toward Victory:

Step 1:

Acknowledge Your Fear—Admit that you're afraid of what others might think.

Step 2:

Reframe Judgment—Shift your focus from external validation to self-fulfillment.

Step 3:

Embrace Imperfection—Understand that even the most successful people have faced judgment along their journey.

2. IMPOSTER SYNDROME

Definition:

Imposter syndrome is a psychological phenomenon where individuals doubt their abilities and feel like frauds, despite evidence of their competence and achievements.

Description:

Imposter syndrome can be a familiar feeling – that nagging doubt that despite your achievements, you don't quite measure up. You might find yourself holding back when exploring self-employment, feeling like you're not "officially" qualified, even when your talents and skills suggest otherwise. It may cause you to downplay your skills and hesitate to take action due to an irrational fear of being exposed as a fraud.

Steps Toward Victory:

Step 1:
Recognize the Syndrome—Acknowledge that feeling like a fraud is a common experience.

Step 2:

Celebrate Your Achievements—List your accomplishments and remind yourself of your competence.

Step 3:

Seek Support—Share your feelings with a mentor or trusted friend who can provide reassurance.

3. RISK AVERSION

Definition:

Risk aversion is the tendency to avoid taking risks and prefer safety and certainty, even when potential rewards may outweigh the risks.

Description:

For you, risk aversion might translate to a reluctance to take the leap into self-employment. The prospect of leaving the stability of a traditional job can trigger anxieties about financial security and potential failure, making it challenging to embrace entrepreneurial opportunities.

Steps Toward Victory:

Step 1:
Understand the Power of Risk—Realize that risks often lead to the most significant rewards.

Step 2:
Create a Risk Plan—Analyze potential outcomes and develop contingency plans.

Step 3:
Start Small—Begin with manageable risks, gradually increasing your comfort level.

4. PROCRASTINATION

Definition:
Procrastination is the act of delaying or postponing tasks, often out of avoidance or resistance to getting started.

Description:
Procrastination can sometimes sneak into your life, causing delays in taking crucial steps toward self-employment. The apprehension of making mistakes or encountering obstacles

might lead to postponing essential tasks and create a pattern of avoidance behavior.

Steps Toward Victory:

Step 1:
Identify Your Procrastination Triggers—Recognize what's causing you to delay action.

Step 2:
Set Clear Goals—Create a specific, achievable, and time-bound plan of action.

Step 3:
Take the First Step—Overcome inertia by taking that initial, manageable step.

5. SELF-DOUBT

Definition:
Self-doubt is a lack of confidence in one's abilities or decisions, resulting in uncertainty and questioning of one's own potential for success.

Description:
Self-doubt might hit home, and that inner critic often whispers doubts about your abilities and decisions. When considering self-employment, it can become a stumbling block, making you question your readiness and your potential for financial independence through your entrepreneurial journey.

Steps Toward Victory:

Step 1:
Challenge Negative Self-Talk—Replace self-criticism with positive affirmations.

Step 2:
Document Your Successes—Maintain a record of your accomplishments and achievements.

Step 3:
Seek Feedback and Validation—Reach out to mentors, colleagues, or peers who can provide constructive feedback and reassurance.

The Inspiring Story of Sir Edmund Hillary

Sir Edmund Hillary, a renowned New Zealand mountaineer, embarked on a challenging quest to become the first person to summit Mount Everest–the highest mountain in the world. The initial chapter of his journey was marked by monumental failures. His first attempt to conquer the formidable peak concluded in disappointment, but rather than succumbing to the fear of failure, Hillary saw it as an invaluable learning experience. Undeterred by setbacks, he meticulously analyzed his mistakes and used them as stepping stones toward improvement. This period of reflection and dedication laid the foundation for the subsequent chapters of his remarkable story.

Fueled by an unwavering determination, Hillary forged ahead on his quest to conquer Everest. Each setback became a lesson, each failure a catalyst for growth. His persistence paid off when, after overcoming numerous challenges, he stood triumphantly atop the world's highest peak. Hillary's narrative serves as a poignant reminder that the fear of failure is an inherent aspect of any journey. What distinguishes the triumphant from the defeated is not the absence of fear, but rather the resilience to confront it head-on and the willingness to extract wisdom from every setback. In the end, Hillary's ascent of Mount Everest became a testament to the transformative power of persistence, dedication, and the ability to turn failures into stepping stones toward ultimate success.

REFLECTION

CHAPTER 8

THE POWER OF NETWORKING

Building Your Professional Circle

CHAPTER 8

THE POWER OF NETWORKING
Building Your Professional Circle

"Your network is your net worth."
Porter Gale

"Succeeding in business is all about making the right connections."
Richard Branson

"The richest people in the world look for and build networks, everyone else looks for work."
Robert Kiyosaki

Professional networking is more than just a fancy buzzword; it's the secret formula of business and opportunity growth. In a world where opportunities are often unlocked by who you know, nurturing your network becomes an invaluable golden ticket. It's all about creating connections, sharing insights, swapping stories, and collaborating with like-minded individuals to build your support team and discover new opportunities.

Wait, there's more! Here's the magic of networking: it's not just about the number of business cards you collect or LinkedIn connections you make. It's the equity of the relationships you build that truly counts. The mentors who offer wisdom, the colleagues who become collaborators, and the friends who become your fans—they all contribute to your professional net worth.

It's a wealth that extends beyond dollars and cents, representing a treasure chest of knowledge, a safety net of support, and a journal of shared experiences that money can't buy.

Here are EIGHT Ways to Begin Building Your Networking Circle:

1. Attend Networking Events

Start by participating in industry-related conferences, seminars, and meetups. These gatherings provide an excellent platform to meet like-minded professionals. Many of these events have social media groups that are an additional way to extend the connection and community, as well as stay informed on when the events are happening.

2. Leverage Social Media

Utilize platforms like LinkedIn, X, Facebook, and Instagram to connect with individuals in your field and engage in relevant discussions; however, don't limit yourself to specific social media sites. Stay relevant.

3. Join Professional Associations

Become a member of industry-specific organizations that offer networking opportunities, such as conferences, webinars, and local chapter events. This might be an industry specific group or even your local chamber of commerce. In my experience, these groups are challenging to get your foot in the door when it comes to professional relationships; however, the best thing to do is bring value to the table. Many of these groups have members who have been in their field for decades and worked hard to earn where they are. Show honor. Bring value. Seek to give and not receive.

4. Seek Mentorship

Identify experienced professionals who can offer guidance and insights, and ask if they would be willing to mentor you. I have found that many leaders love to mentor, but they don't like wasting their time. Offer an exchange for the mentorship—a fee for their time, a profit share, a small equity position, or even as simple as you will buy their lunch every time you meet.

5. Build Your Online Presence

Create a personal website or podcast to

showcase your expertise and interests. Sharing valuable content can attract connections. The more value you bring, the more your network will expand and your business will grow. This needs to be in conjunction with your social media platform. People consume most of their content via the Internet—to be relevant, you must be present.

6. Offer Your Help

Volunteer or assist others within your industry. Offering your skills or time can establish you as a valuable and dependable member of your professional community. I had a mentor once tell me that one of the best ways up is to serve your way into success. The law of the harvest—you must sow if you want to reap; you must give if you want to receive. Selfishness isn't sustainable.

7. Explore Networking Apps

Discover platforms designed for networking to help you connect with professionals. Engage by offering free tips, tricks, or advice.

8. Follow Up and Maintain Contacts

After meeting new connections, follow up with a friendly message or an invitation for a coffee or virtual chat. Maintaining relationships is as important as creating them. Your relationships are only as healthy as the care you give to them. Here's the good news: professional relationships are not personal relationships. They require much less energy and effort to maintain, but they cannot be ignored or neglected.

Gary Vee's Perspective on Networking

In the world of networking, Gary Vaynerchuk, better known as Gary Vee, is a prominent voice. He emphasizes the power of authenticity in building connections. According to him, networking isn't about exchanging business cards or collecting contacts; it's about creating real, meaningful relationships. In an era of digital communication, he encourages professionals to prioritize human connections, reminding us that it's not the quantity but the quality of our network that truly counts. Gary Vee's approach teaches us that genuine relationships in our

professional circle can be a conduit to success,
as they bring not just opportunities, but the
trust and support of a community.

REFLECTION

CHAPTER 9

MONEY MATTERS

Financial Freedom and Streams of Income

CHAPTER 9

MONEY MATTERS
Financial Freedom and Streams of Income

Financial independence is a goal many strive for, but often find elusive. It's a state of financial security that allows you to maintain your desired lifestyle without the need for employment income. Shockingly, a significant portion of Americans face financial insecurity, with studies indicating that a considerable percentage wouldn't be able to handle an unexpected expense of $400 without financial stress. For most Americans, reaching financial independence remains a significant challenge. The idea of retirement isn't merely tied to age; it's about achieving a specific financial milestone that provides the freedom to retire comfortably.

The Power of Passive Income

Achieving lasting financial freedom is a noble pursuit that hinges on the transformative concept of passive income. At its core, passive income entails earning money with minimal ongoing effort, a mechanism that liberates individuals from the shackles of traditional nine-to-five employment. This paradigm shift allows for the cultivation of wealth beyond the constraints of time, offering a pathway to financial independence that is both inspiring and achievable.

One of the key elements of passive income is the requirement for an initial investment or effort, laying the foundation for a self-sustaining financial ecosystem. For instance, investing in rental properties or dividend-yielding assets demands an upfront commitment but opens doors to perpetual earnings. This initial dedication serves as the catalyst for a cascading stream of income, fostering a sense of security and empowerment. The essence of passive income lies in the wisdom of planting seeds today that will bear fruit tomorrow, creating a legacy of financial stability that lasts for generations.

Furthermore, the diverse avenues through which passive income can be generated add to its allure. Beyond traditional investments, revenue streams from royalties and online ventures, such as blogs or YouTube channels, exemplify the adaptability of this financial philosophy.

The ability to monetize creativity and expertise extends the reach of passive income, making it accessible to a wide array of individuals. As these income streams flow in, detached from the direct exchange of time for money, a profound sense of liberation emerges, fostering a mindset shift toward the limitless possibilities of financial prosperity.

In essence, embracing the concept of passive income is not just a financial strategy; it is a mindset that propels individuals towards a life of abundance and fulfillment. By understanding and implementing the principles of passive income, one not only secures a reliable financial future but also embarks on a journey of self-discovery and empowerment, creating a legacy that transcends monetary wealth alone.

The Magic of Multiple Streams of Income

Creating multiple streams of income is a strategic approach that goes beyond mere financial management—it's a pathway to reducing risk and unlocking the doors to wealth. Imagine your income not as a singular flow but as a dynamic network, with each stream contributing to a river of financial prosperity. This approach involves diversifying your revenue sources, encompassing not just your primary job but also delving into side businesses, smart investments, and the power of passive income. It's the art of building a robust financial portfolio, much like a skilled artist blends colors on a canvas to create a masterpiece.

One key advantage of cultivating multiple streams of income is the liberation it provides from the shackles of dependency on a single source. While a full-time job may be the foundation, exploring entrepreneurial endeavors or investment opportunities becomes the pillars that support your financial structure. Just as a well-designed house distributes its weight evenly, a diversified income portfolio distributes financial risk, creating a safety net that shields you from the unpredictable winds of economic change. This safety net not only fosters stability but also serves as a launchpad for future financial endeavors, allowing you to take calculated risks and pursue opportunities that align with your goals.

Moreover, the beauty of this approach lies in its adaptability to various life stages and goals. Whether you aspire to retire early, travel the world, or support a cause close to your heart, multiple streams of income empower you to design a life of purpose and abundance. It's a journey where each stream becomes a tributary feeding into the river of your dreams, propelling you forward with the momentum of financial freedom. As you weave these streams together, you're not just securing your present; you're architecting a future that transcends the limitations of a singular income source. Embrace the power of diversity in income, and witness the transformation of your financial landscape into a masterpiece of abundance and security.

Here are EIGHT Ways to Reach Financial Independence:

1. Entrepreneurship

While many individuals can reach financial independence in their lifetimes by working a career, very few career-only individuals can retire early. In fact, almost all billionaires achieved this high level of financial success through entrepreneurial efforts. Starting a business can be a path to financial independence. It provides the opportunity to create income and build wealth by pursuing your passions.

2. Investments

Building an investment portfolio can be a long-term strategy for growing your wealth. Investments in stocks, mutual funds, bonds, and other assets can contribute to financial independence. On their own, these tools will generally take decades to compound enough to help you reach your financial freedom number.

3. Diversify Your Income Sources

Exploring additional income streams, such as side jobs or freelance work, allows you to reduce reliance on a single source of income. Many freelancers find that the gig economy affords them a lot of flexibility and freedom to work on their own timeframe and from any-where in the world. This project-to-project based approach allows you to not be tied down or overly committed to any single organization.

4. Budgeting

A well-structured budget helps manage expenses and maximize savings. It's an essential tool for achieving financial independence. At the end of the day, financial independence isn't about how much money you make. It's about how much money you keep! Take control of your spending or it will control you. My grandfather used to say, "Take care of the pennies and the dollars take care of themselves." Keep track of where your money is going, look for your spending leaks, and get serious about living below your means.

5. Continuous Learning

Investing in your skills and knowledge can increase your earning potential and adaptability in a changing financial landscape. In this modern era of technology, things change quickly. Stay up to speed on new advancements and ideas. Also, if your money is working for you passively, then you need to focus on learning a little bit about that industry. I only invest in areas about which I have learned. It's hard to get scammed if you have done the research. Never stop learning.

6. Real Estate Investments

Investing in real estate can be a substantial path to financial independence. I love real estate—from rental properties to flipping houses. Owning rental properties can provide a consistent stream of income and long-term wealth appreciation. Additionally, real estate investments can offer tax advantages, and these tax benefits can help maximize your income and minimize your tax liability; however, successful real estate investing requires research, financial planning, and a long-term perspective. While it may not provide immediate financial independence, real estate can be a robust path to building substantial wealth and achieving financial security over time.

7. Create and Sell Intellectual Property

If you possess creative talents, consider creating intellectual property such as books, music, software, or artwork. Earnings from royalties and licensing agreements can provide passive income over time. Oftentimes, these products take some initial time and financial investment; however, when created into digital products, they live on forever.

8. Automate and Scale Your Business

If you're an entrepreneur or business owner, focus on automating processes and scaling your operations. This can increase your revenue and free up your time, moving you closer to financial independence. Don't leave a career path only to start your own job—start a business, run a system. If you aren't careful, then your business will become a job. Begin with your freedom in mind, otherwise you will live out your days trapped in an unhealthy whirlpool of your new nightmare. Plan your exit. Make the system work for you.

Achieving financial independence is a commendable endeavor that demands meticulous planning, prudent financial choices, and a steadfast commitment to establishing diverse income streams. The path to financial freedom involves not only earning money but also managing it wisely. By strategically diversifying your sources of income and actively engaging in financial education, you position yourself to make consistent strides toward the coveted goal of financial independence.

Embracing the principles of financial literacy is essential in navigating the complexities of personal finance. Cultivating a deep understanding of budgeting, investing, and wealth-building strategies empowers individuals to make informed decisions that contribute to their financial well-being. As you embrace these practices, you pave the way for a more secure

and self-reliant financial future, ultimately steering yourself towards the realization of financial
independence.

REFLECTION

____

____

____

____

____

____

____

____

CONCLUSION

RECLAIMING YOUR FUTURE

Your Guide to Ditching the Career

CONCLUSION

RECLAIMING YOUR FUTURE
Your Guide to Ditching the Career

As we close the pages of "Ditch the Career: Shattering Myths and Unlocking Your Potential," it's essential to reflect on the journey we've undertaken together. We embarked on this exploration of reclaiming your future, questioning the traditional career narrative, and daring to imagine a life unburdened by the constraints of the past.

In Part 1, we unmasked the common myths that keep us from taking the revolutionary steps to change our lives. We confronted the career trap, which often shackles us to a desk, leaving our dreams to languish in the shadows. We've seen that the 9-to-5 paradigm and the belief in the necessity of a college degree are myths that hinder our pursuit of true success. Climbing the corporate ladder, while often perceived as a path to greatness, can sometimes lead us to the precipice of disillusionment.

In Part 2, we discovered alternative paths. Freelancing and embracing the digital nomad lifestyle are both viable ways to escape the constraints of the traditional office. We also explored the age-old debate of passion versus paycheck, learning that it's possible to turn your interests into a fulfilling career.

Part 3 explored the inner and outer aspects of achieving your potential. Overcoming the fear of failure is a critical step in this journey, and we learned that building a network of like-minded individuals can be a catalyst for success. Finally, we recognized that financial independence and diversifying your income streams are crucial for taking control of your destiny.

Now, armed with knowledge and insight, you stand at a crossroads. You have the choice to reject the career mold and forge your path, unburdened by misconceptions and societal pressure. You can dare to dream, unshackling your potential and embracing a future where passion, purpose, and prosperity converge.

Here are SIX Concluding Action Steps You can take as a Blueprint for Success in Ditching Your Career and Pursuing a More Fulfilling Path

1. Self-Reflect and Set Goals

Take the time to reflect on your passions, values, and what truly motivates you. Set clear, achievable goals for your desired future, both short-term and long-term. This will serve as your roadmap for success.

2. Become Focused on Growth

Embrace a growth mindset and commit to lifelong learning. This may include acquiring new skills, reading books, attending workshops, taking online courses, or seeking mentors who can guide you on your chosen path.

3. Build Your Network

Actively grow your professional network. Attend industry events, join online communities, and engage with like-minded individuals who share your interests and aspirations. These connections can open doors to opportunities and provide valuable support.

4. Financial Planning

Develop a robust financial plan that allows you to sustain your lifestyle while transitioning away from a traditional career. Consider creating multiple income streams, saving and investing wisely, and ensuring you have a financial safety net in place.

5. Make Wise Decisions

Recognize that moving away from the career mold often involves stepping out of your comfort zone. You need to make wise, calculated decisions. Be willing to take calculated risks and embrace change, but don't be completely foolish. This might mean starting a side gig, freelancing, or relocating to explore new opportunities.

6. Don't Give Up

Understand that the journey to ditching your career and pursuing your dreams can be challenging. Stay resilient in the face of setbacks and obstacles. Keep a positive mindset, learn from failures, and use them as stepping stones to future success.

Remember, the path to success outside the traditional career trajectory is a unique and personal journey. It will require determination, adaptability, and a commitment to your vision. These action steps can serve as a blueprint for your success, guiding you as you reclaim your future and chart your own course to fulfillment and prosperity.

Keep in mind, your future is not a one-size-fits-all mold, and the path you choose may not resemble anyone else's. It's unique to you, just as your dreams and ambitions are.

As you move forward, apply the lessons from this book, but also remember that the real power to reclaim your future lies within you.

Now you are ready! Take off with courage, resilience, and a burning desire to create a life that aligns with your aspirations.

Embrace the unknown, explore the possibilities, and may your journey be one of fulfillment, joy, and the realization of your dreams.

Your future is yours to reclaim and redefine. So, ditch the career and unlock your full potential!

KEY TAKEAWAYS FROM THE BOOK

BONUS

THE 30 DAY ENTREPRENEUR CHALLENGE

Discover Your Talents, Passions, and Dreams

MAXIMIZING THE CHALLENGE
What You Need to do to Prepare
for this 30 Day Challenge

1]. You need to cultivate a mindset of commitment. Don't begin this and not finish. Don't skip a day. Set aside the time each morning to invest in you.

2]. You need to engage in daily self-reflection exercises, such as journaling about personal achievements, moments of fulfillment, and activities that bring joy, sets the foundation for understanding one's intrinsic motivations. This introspective approach allows individuals to identify patterns, values, and themes that may align with potential entrepreneurial pursuits.

3]. You need to embrace a growth mindset. Entrepreneurs should view challenges as opportunities for learning and be open to adapting their perspectives throughout the journey. This mental preparedness is essential for the transformative experience the challenge aims to provide.

THE FORMAT:

SOW - read the daily content from this book

KNOW - take 10 minutes to read a book that will help your leadership, growth, or knowledge

GROW - take 10 minutes to journal

SHOW - complete the challenge before you go to bed

WHAT DO YOU NEED:

1. This book, of course

2. A journal (physical or digital) to document your growth

3. Additional resources (books, ariticles, etc) for the daily reading.

4. Accountability. You need to ask someone to be an accountability mentor that you will send an email or text to every 5 days with a brief update on how you are progressing.

THE COMMITMENT

Before we begin, you will need to make a commitment to yourself. Each day is important. The daily challenges matter. So, there are 4 commitments you must make before beginning this 30-day journey. If you agree to these commitments, initial beside them. Then, at the bottom of this page, sign your pledge.

1. I commit to completing each day : _______

2. I commit to 10 minutes of reading : _______

3. I commit to 10 minutes of reflection : _______

4. I commit to completing the action step : _______

I pledge to complete this 30 day challenge:

____
Signature

____
Date

DAY

1

SELF-REFLECTION

SOW - See Page 121

KNOW - take 10 minutes today to read a book to help your leadership, growth, or knowledge

GROW - take 10 minutes to journal

SHOW - complete the challenge before you go to bed

SELF-REFLECTION

ACTION:
Grab some paper. Write about your life journey. Consider key milestones, achievements, and moments that brought you fulfillment. Reflect on challenges you've overcome and the lessons you've learned using the following actions steps:

Values Identification:
List five values that are most important to you. These could be principles that have guided your decisions and actions throughout your life.

Passion Inventory:
Make a list of activities that genuinely excite you and make you lose track of time. Identify common themes or patterns in these activities.

Goals Setting:
Write down three short-term and three long-term goals you have for yourself. These goals can be personal or professional, and they will serve as initial guideposts for your entrepreneurial journey.

Positive Affirmation:
End your reflection by writing a positive affirmation about your potential and the journey ahead. This affirmation will serve as a motivational mantra throughout the challenge.

Outcome:
This day is about laying the foundation for your entrepreneurial exploration. By delving into your own experiences, values, passions, and goals, you'll gain a clearer understanding of your intrinsic motivations and set the stage for uncovering potential business ideas that align with your authentic self.

DAY 2

STRENGTHS UNVEILING

SOW - See Page 123

KNOW - take 10 minutes today to read a book to help your leadership, growth, or knowledge

GROW - take 10 minutes to journal

SHOW - complete the challenge before you go to bed

STRENGTHS UNVEILING

ACTION:
Identify and leverage your unique strengths for entrepreneurial success.

Strengths Assessment:
Take a strengths assessment test (e.g., Gallup StrengthsFinder) to pinpoint your core strengths.

Reflection:
Analyze the results and consider how you can apply your strengths to entrepreneurial endeavors.

Skill Alignment:
Identify specific skills associated with your strengths and brainstorm how these skills can contribute to your business ideas.

Goal Setting:
Set a goal for leveraging at least one of your strengths in a new or enhanced way within the next month.

Outcome:
By understanding and leveraging your strengths, you'll be better equipped to excel in your entrepreneurial journey and capitalize on what sets you apart.

DAY
3

PASSION EXPLORATION

SOW - See Page 125

KNOW - take 10 minutes today to read a book to help your leadership, growth, or knowledge

GROW - take 10 minutes to journal

SHOW - complete the challenge before you go to bed

PASSION EXPLORATION

ACTION:
Today, I want you to deeper into your passions to uncover potential business ideas.

Activity Analysis:
Review the list of activities from Day 1 that brought you joy. Identify the top three activities that resonate the most with you.

Passion Mapping:
Create a visual map or diagram connecting these activities and exploring potential intersections that could lead to business ideas.

Research:
Spend 10-15 minutes today researching industries or businesses related to your identified passions.

Networking:
Reach out to someone in a field aligned with your passions for a brief conversation or informational interview. Consider scheduling a time to buy them a cup of coffee or maybe even lunch.

Outcome:
By exploring your passions, you're not only aligning your business ideas with your interests but also setting the stage for a more fulfilling entrepreneurial journey.

DAY
4

YOUR BUCKET LIST

SOW - See Page 127

KNOW - take 10 minutes today to read a book to help your leadership, growth, or knowledge

GROW - take 10 minutes to journal

SHOW - complete the challenge before you go to bed

YOUR BUCKET LIST

ACTION:
Today, you are going to visualize your entrepreneurial dreams through starting your bucket list. I want you to think about what your life could look like if all your dreams came true. Now, while I think a personal bucket list is great, this is designed for your entrepreneurial dreams.

Business Comparisons :
When you look at successful leaders and businesses that resonate with your entrepreneurial vision, which businesses stand out. Make a list of 5-6 businesses that you wnat to model your business after and explain why.

Bucket List Business:
Write down at least 25 big dreams and ambitions you hope you will accomplish through your business. (make $1M, hire over 100 people, retire my parents, etc)

Reflection:
Spend 10 minutes reflecting on your business bucket list. What patterns or themes emerge? How do these lists align with your aspirations?

Personal Bucket List:
I think it is also important to have a personal bucket list. In fact, I have created a bucket list journal that you can purshase on AMAZON called "**The Bucket List Journal: Living an Adventurous Life**" that can be found at the following link:

https://a.co/d/azfQuVq

Outcome:
Your business bucket list will serve as a powerful reminder of your entrepreneurial dreams, fostering motivation and clarity.

DAY 5

SKILL DEVELOPMENT

SOW - See Page 129

KNOW - take 10 minutes today to read a book to help your leadership, growth, or knowledge

GROW - take 10 minutes to journal

SHOW - complete the challenge before you go to bed. Text your accountability mentor.

SKILL DEVELOPMENT

ACTION:
Plan the development of skills crucial for your entrepreneurial journey.

Skills Identification:
List three skills essential for your business idea or industry.

Resource Exploration:
Research online courses, workshops, or books that can help you acquire or enhance these skills.

Learning Schedule:
Create a schedule outlining when and how you'll dedicate time to skill development.

Implementation:
Commit to starting the learning process for at least one of the identified skills.

Outcome:
Developing relevant skills is integral to entrepreneurial success. This plan sets the stage for continuous learning and improvement.

DAY

6

YOUR NETWORK

SOW - See Page 131

KNOW - take 10 minutes today to read a book to help your leadership, growth, or knowledge

GROW - take 10 minutes to journal

SHOW - complete the challenge before you go to bed

YOUR NETWORK

ACTION:
Begin building your entrepreneurial network.

LinkedIn Profile:
Create or enhance your LinkedIn profile to reflect your entrepreneurial interests and aspirations.

Connection Outreach:
Send connection requests to at least two professionals in your field of interest with a personalized message expressing your eagerness to learn.

Online Community Joining:
Identify and join an online community or forum related to entrepreneurship.

Engagement:
Contribute to a discussion or share valuable insights within your chosen online community.

Outcome:
Building a robust network is a vital aspect of entrepreneurship, offering opportunities for mentorship, collaboration, and learning from others' experiences.

DAY
7

CLARITY & FOCUS

SOW - See Page 133

KNOW - take 10 minutes today to read a book to help your leadership, growth, or knowledge

GROW - take 10 minutes to journal

SHOW - complete the challenge before you go to bed

CLARITY & FOCUS

ACTION:
Today is all about building mental strength. We are goint to focus on cultivating mindfulness to gain clarity and focus. So, today is all about slowing down.

Mindful Breathing:
Spend 10 minutes practicing mindful breathing. Focus on your breath, allowing thoughts to come and go without judgment.

Gratitude Journaling:
Write down 5-10 things you're grateful for in relation to your entrepreneurial journey.

Goal Visualization:
Visualize the successful achievement of one of your entrepreneurial goals. Focus on what you can do today to start making that happen.

Mindfulness Routine:
Plan a daily mindfulness routine, integrating practices such as meditation, prayer, or mindful walks.

Outcome:
Mindfulness fosters clarity, enabling you to approach your entrepreneurial journey with focus, resilience, and a positive mindset.

DAY
8

RISK TOLERANCE

SOW - See Page 135

KNOW - take 10 minutes today to read a book to help your leadership, growth, or knowledge

GROW - take 10 minutes to journal

SHOW - complete the challenge before you go to bed

RISK TOLERANCE

ACTION:
Evaluate your risk tolerance in the context of entrepreneurial endeavors.

Risk Identification:
List potential risks associated with starting and running your own business.

Personal Assessment:
Reflect on your comfort level with uncertainty and your ability to navigate challenges.

Risk Mitigation Strategies:
Develop strategies for mitigating or managing the identified risks.

Commitment Statement:
Write a commitment statement expressing your willingness to embrace calculated risks on your entrepreneurial journey.

Outcome:
Understanding and accepting risk is crucial in entrepreneurship. This exercise prepares you to face challenges with resilience and strategic thinking.

DAY

9

SELF-DISCIPLINE

SOW - See Page 137

KNOW - take 10 minutes today to read a book to help your leadership, growth, or knowledge

GROW - take 10 minutes to journal

SHOW - complete the challenge before you go to bed

SELF-DISCIPLINE

ACTION:
Discipline is the key to unlocking your entrepreneurial future. Today, you are going to evaluate and strengthen your self-discipline, a crucial trait for entrepreneurial success.

Reflect on Commitments:
Review your current commitments and goals. Identify areas where self-discipline has played a role in your achievements.

Time Management Analysis:
Assess how effectively you manage your time. Identify time-wasting habits and areas for improvement.

Goal Consistency:
Evaluate your consistency in pursuing your goals. Reflect on instances where you demonstrated strong self-discipline and areas for enhancement.

Distraction Identification:
Identify common distractions that hinder your productivity. Develop strategies to minimize or eliminate these distractions.

Self-Discipline Plan:
Create a self-discipline plan outlining specific steps to enhance your ability to stay focused, manage time efficiently, and consistently work towards your goals.

Outcome:
A strong foundation of self-discipline is essential for navigating the challenges of entrepreneurship. This day focuses on self-awareness and strategic planning to strengthen your self-discipline for sustained success.

DAY
10

YOUR ELEVATOR PITCH

SOW - See Page 139

KNOW - take 10 minutes today to read a book to help your leadership, growth, or knowledge

GROW - take 10 minutes to journal

SHOW - complete the challenge before you go to bed. Text your accountability mentor.

YOUR ELEVATOR PITCH

ACTION:
Today, I want you to develop a concise and compelling elevator pitch for your business. You never know who you might meet. If you only have a moment to make a quick-pitch, then you want to be prepared.

Define Your Value:
Clearly articulate the unique value proposition of your business in one sentence. I call this your impact statement.

Target Audience Inclusion:
Specify your target audience and write down why they would benefit from your product or service.

Putting the Pitch Together:
Write one sentence regarding each of these 5 areas and keep it clear and concise:
1. Introduce Yourself
2. What's Your Experience?
3. What is the Problem You are Solving?
4. How are You Going to Solve It?
5. What is the Call to Action?

Practice Session:
Rehearse your elevator pitch in front of a mirror or with a friend. Aim for clarity and simplicity.

Refinement:
Based on feedback, refine your pitch to make it more impactful and memorable.

Outcome:
An effective elevator pitch is a powerful tool for introducing your business to potential partners, investors, or customers succinctly and compellingly.

DAY

11

FINANCIAL EDUCATION

SOW - See Page 141

KNOW - take 10 minutes today to read a book to help your leadership, growth, or knowledge

GROW - take 10 minutes to journal

SHOW - complete the challenge before you go to bed

FINANCIAL EDUCATION

ACTION:
Enhance your understanding of financial concepts relevant to entrepreneurship.

Basic Financial Concepts:
Familiarize yourself with fundamental financial terms such as revenue, expenses, profit, and cash flow.

Budget Creation:
Develop a basic budget for your business, outlining anticipated expenses and potential income.

Financial Resources:
Identify online resources, courses, or books that can deepen your financial knowledge.

Consultation:
Consider seeking advice from a financial advisor or mentor to gain personalized insights.

Outcome:
A solid understanding of financial principles is crucial for effective business planning and sustainable growth.

DAY 12

FAILING FORWARD

SOW - See Page 143

KNOW - take 10 minutes today to read a book to help your leadership, growth, or knowledge

GROW - take 10 minutes to journal

SHOW - complete the challenge before you go to bed

FAILING FORWARD

ACTION:
Today is all about embracing failure as a learning opportunity. Shift your perspective on failure and view it as a stepping stone to success.

Failure Reflection:
Recall a specific instance of failure in your life or career and identify the lessons learned.

Mindset Shift:
Acknowledge that failure is a natural part of the entrepreneurial journey and an opportunity for growth.

Failure as Feedback:
Consider how feedback from failures can contribute to the refinement of your business ideas. We are our biggest critics. When you have a failure, offer yourself some constructive feedback.

Positive Affirmation:
Develop a positive affirmation related to resilience and learning from setbacks.

Outcome:
Embracing failure as a teacher fosters a resilient mindset, enabling you to navigate challenges with a constructive attitude.

DAY

13

PROTOTYPE YOUR IDEA

SOW - See Page 145

KNOW - take 10 minutes today to read a book to help your leadership, growth, or knowledge

GROW - take 10 minutes to journal

SHOW - complete the challenge before you go to bed

PROTOTYPE YOUR IDEA

ACTION:
Bring your business idea to life through a basic prototype.

Idea Outline:
Outline the key features and benefits of your business idea.

Sketch or Mockup:
Create a simple visual representation, either by sketching on paper or using digital tools. Whether it is a product or service, use either sketches or word pictures to create a visualized mockup.

Feedback Gathering:
Share your prototype with a friend, family member, or mentor, and gather feedback.

Iteration:
Based on feedback, make necessary adjustments and refine your prototype.

Outcome:
Prototyping allows you to visualize your idea and gather valuable insights early in the development process.

DAY 14

PERSONAL BRANDING

SOW - See Page 147

KNOW - take 10 minutes today to read a book to help your leadership, growth, or knowledge

GROW - take 10 minutes to journal

SHOW - complete the challenge before you go to bed

PERSONAL BRANDING

ACTION:
Define and articulate your personal brand for entrepreneurial success.

Core Values Identification:
Revisit your list of core values from Day 1 and use them as a foundation for your personal brand. After 2 weeks, has anything changed? How do these values support your perosnal brand?

Brand Statement:
Craft a concise and compelling personal brand statement that communicates who you are and what you stand for.

Interview Yourself:
Imagine that you are interviewing yourself to find out about who you are and your brand. Make a list of 10 questions you would ask yourself. Then, answer those questions to give yourself a good baseline for explaining your brand.

Online Presence Update:
After 2 weeks in this challenge, it is time to update your LinkedIn profile and other professional platforms to reflect your refined personal brand. Also, take 5 minutes today to try to network with some new connections.

Outcome:
A strong personal brand enhances your credibility and visibility, setting the stage for entrepreneurial success.

DAY
15

SOCIAL MEDIA

SOW - See Page 149

KNOW - take 10 minutes today to read a book to help your leadership, growth, or knowledge

GROW - take 10 minutes to journal

SHOW - complete the challenge before you go to bed. Text your accountability mentor.

SOCIAL MEDIA

ACTION:
Establish a strong online presence for your entrepreneurial journey. Regardless of your age, you need a strong social media presence if you want to be relevant as an entrepreneur.

Platform Selection:
Choose the social media platforms most relevant to your industry and target audience. You MUST be where your audience is.

Content Strategy:
Develop a content strategy outlining the type of content you'll share, the frequency, and the messaging. On average, most entrepreneurs don't spend enough time leveraging social media for business and they don't post frequently enough.

Engagement Plan:
Plan how you will engage with your audience, including responding to comments, sharing valuable content, and participating in relevant discussions. Will you engage through videos or written posts? I suggest both.

Consistency:
Commit to a consistent posting schedule and engagement plan for the next month. Make a daily business engagement on 2-3 different platforms and watch how it changes your impact.

Outcome:
A strategic and consistent social media presence helps build your brand, connect with your audience, and establish yourself as a thought leader in your field.

DAY

16

MENTORSHIP

SOW - See Page 151

KNOW - take 10 minutes today to read a book to help your leadership, growth, or knowledge

GROW - take 10 minutes to journal

SHOW - complete the challenge before you go to bed

MENTORSHIP

ACTION:
Connect with a mentor to gain valuable insights for your entrepreneurial journey.

Mentor Identification:
Make a list of 4-5 leaders in your industry or a related field whom you admire and respect.

Outreach:
Reach out to at least one of the potential mentors with a thoughtful message expressing your admiration and seeking mentorship. Remember, seek to give value if you want to receive mentorship.

Meeting Setup:
If a mentor agrees, schedule a virtual or in-person meeting to discuss your entrepreneurial goals. Treat them to lunch or coffee if they agree to meet in person.

Questions Preparation:
Prepare a list of specific questions about their experiences and advice. Be efficient and considerate with their time.

Outcome:
Building a mentor-mentee relationship provides invaluable guidance, support, and a unique perspective to navigate challenges.

DAY 17

TIME MANAGEMENT

SOW - See Page 153

KNOW - take 10 minutes today to read a book to help your leadership, growth, or knowledge

GROW - take 10 minutes to journal

SHOW - complete the challenge before you go to bed

TIME MANAGEMENT

ACTION:
Develop effective time management skills for entrepreneurial success.

Time Audit:
Track your activities for a day to identify time-wasting habits and opportunities for improvement.

Prioritization:
Create a daily to-do list, prioritizing tasks based on urgency and importance.

Time Blocking:
Allocate specific blocks of time for focused work, minimizing multi-tasking.

Reflection:
End the day by reflecting on what worked well and where you can improve in managing your time.

Outcome:
Efficient time management is essential for balancing various aspects of entrepreneurship and maximizing productivity.

DAY

18

EMBRACING FEEDBACK

SOW - See Page 155

KNOW - take 10 minutes today to read a book to help your leadership, growth, or knowledge

GROW - take 10 minutes to journal

SHOW - complete the challenge before you go to bed

EMBRACING FEEDBACK

ACTION:
Foster a culture of continuous improvement through feedback.

Feedback Solicitation:
Request feedback from a colleague, friend, or mentor regarding your entrepreneurial ideas or plans.

Reflective Listening:
Actively listen to the feedback without immediate judgment. Take notes on constructive points.

Feedback Implementation:
Create a list of specific actions you can take to address the feedback and enhance your plans.

Feedback Loop:
Commit to regularly seeking and integrating feedback throughout your entrepreneurial journey.

Outcome:
Embracing feedback as a constructive tool fosters personal and professional growth, improving your ideas and strategies.

DAY

19

STARTING A BUSINESS

SOW - See Page 157

KNOW - take 10 minutes today to read a book to help your leadership, growth, or knowledge

GROW - take 10 minutes to journal

SHOW - complete the challenge before you go to bed

STARTING A BUSINESS

ACTION:
Grab some paper. Today, you are going to dive into the fundamental aspects of launching and running a successful business

Regulatory Landscape:
Research and list key regulatory considerations when starting a business, including permits, licenses, and compliance requirements. How will you structure your business? Do you need an LLC? How will you do your financials, taxes, etc?

Legal & Financial Consultation:
If possible, consult with a legal professional, CPA, and/or mentor to discuss the legal and financial intricacies associated with your specific business idea.

Business Plan:
Do you have a business plan? If not, create an outline of your business. Answer questions like: who? what? when? where? why? how? Additionally, think about the contracts, agreements, and legal documentation needed.

Next Steps Planning:
Identify the immediate next steps required to establish your business legally and ethically. Share this list with your mentor.

Outcome:
Understanding the legal and regulatory aspects of starting a business is crucial for a smooth and compliant launch, setting the foundation for sustainable growth.

DAY
20

ETHICAL IMPACT

SOW - See Page 159

KNOW - take 10 minutes today to read a book to help your leadership, growth, or knowledge

GROW - take 10 minutes to journal

SHOW - complete the challenge before you go to bed. Text your accountability mentor.

ETHICAL IMPACT

ACTION:
Integrate social and ethical responsibility into your business planning. As a future business leader, you have an opportunity and responsibility to make a positive impact.

Values Alignment:
Ensure your business values align with ethical and socially responsible practices.

Impact Assessment:
Identify ways your business can positively impact the community, environment, or a social cause. Look up ethical and social responsibility statements and values of organizations you respect.

Partnership Exploration:
Research potential partnerships with socially responsible organizations or initiatives.

Action Plan:
Develop a plan to implement at least one socially responsible initiative within your business.

Outcome:
Social responsibility not only contributes to the greater good, but also enhances your business reputation and customer loyalty.

DAY 21

ADAPTABILITY

SOW - See Page 161

KNOW - take 10 minutes today to read a book to help your leadership, growth, or knowledge

GROW - take 10 minutes to journal

SHOW - complete the challenge before you go to bed

ADAPTABILITY

ACTION:
Develop and cultivate adaptability skills to navigate the ever-changing entrepreneurial landscape.

Resilience Reflection:
Reflect on a challenging situation you've faced and consider how you adapted to overcome it. What worked? What didn't work? What would you have changed in how you responded?

Industry Trends Research:
Stay updated on current trends in your industry and explore how you can adapt your business strategies accordingly. Make a list of 1-2 current trends that you can immediately implement into your business.

Scenario Planning:
Identify potential future challenges for your business and develop contingency plans.

Mindset Shift:
Embrace change as an opportunity for growth rather than a hurdle.

Outcome:
Cultivating adaptability allows you to navigate uncertainties and capitalize on opportunities for innovation and growth.

DAY
22

VISION FOR SUCCESS

SOW - See Page 163

KNOW - take 10 minutes today to read a book to help your leadership, growth, or knowledge

GROW - take 10 minutes to journal

SHOW - complete the challenge before you go to bed

VISION FOR SUCCESS

ACTION:
In order for your business to be successful, the vision you have for your business needs to be clear and intentional. If you are going to sell the vision, then you need to fully believe in what you are selling. Today, we are going to concentrate on focusing on your vision–keeping the vision at the forefront of your own mind.

Visualization Exercise:
Spend 10 minutes visualizing your business achieving success. Picture specific scenarios, achievements, and positive outcomes. Make notes about what you love about what you are imagining.

Bucket List Review:
Revisit your business bucket list from Day 4 and reflect on how it aligns with your visualized success.

Affirmations:
Create and repeat positive affirmations related to your envisioned success throughout the day.

Goal Alignment:
Ensure that your daily actions align with the vision you've created for your business.

Outcome:
Keeping your vision fresh is a powerful tool that aligns your mindset with success, promoting confidence and clarity in your entrepreneurial journey.

DAY 23

HEALTH & WELLNESS

SOW - See Page 165

KNOW - take 10 minutes today to read a book to help your leadership, growth, or knowledge

GROW - take 10 minutes to journal

SHOW - complete the challenge before you go to bed

HEALTH & WELLNESS

ACTION:
If you want to maximize your entrepreneurial success, then you need to be healthy. You need to establish a foundation for well-being to sustain entrepreneurial energy.

Wellness Assessment:
Ok, it's time to take an honest assessment of where your health and wellness are. Evaluate your current physical health and mental health habits and make a list of areas that need improvement.

Self-Care Plan:
Create a self-care plan that includes regular exercise, nutritious meals, counseling, and sufficient sleep. What areas are neglected in your health and wellness that need to be prioritized in your plan?

Mind-Body Connection:
Engage in a mindful activity such as exercise, prayer, reflection, or a nature walk.

Accountability Partner:
Share your wellness goals with a friend or family member for mutual support.

Outcome:
Prioritizing health and wellness is crucial for maintaining the energy and resilience needed for entrepreneurial endeavors.

DAY 24

COLLABORATION

SOW - See Page 167

KNOW - take 10 minutes today to read a book to help your leadership, growth, or knowledge

GROW - take 10 minutes to journal

SHOW - complete the challenge before you go to bed

COLLABORATION

ACTION:
Explore collaboration opportunities to enhance your entrepreneurial journey.

Collaborator Identification:
Identify 3-5 potential collaborators or partners who share complementary skills or goals.

Reach Out:
Initiate contact with at least 2 potential collaborators, expressing your interest in collaboration.

Meeting Setup:
Schedule a virtual or in-person meeting to discuss potential collaboration opportunities.

Collaboration Idea:
Brainstorm a collaborative project or initiative that aligns with your business goals.

Outcome:
Collaboration expands your network, brings diverse perspectives, and fosters innovation within your entrepreneurial journey.

DAY 25

PUBLIC SPEAKING

SOW - See Page 169

KNOW - take 10 minutes today to read a book to help your leadership, growth, or knowledge

GROW - take 10 minutes to journal

SHOW - complete the challenge before you go to bed. Text your accountability mentor.

PUBLIC SPEAKING

ACTION:
Sharpen your public speaking abilities for effective communication.

Speech Preparation:
Choose a topic related to your business and prepare a 3-5 minute speech.

Practice & Record Session:
Rehearse your speech in front of a mirror and then record yourself for self-evaluation.

Feedback Gathering:
Share your speech with a friend or family member and gather constructive feedback. Ask them for suggestions regarding your verbal and non-verbal communication skills.

Toastmasters or Similar Group:
If you are an inexperienced public speaker, then consider joining a public speaking group to further hone your skills.

Outcome:
Effective public speaking is a valuable skill for networking, pitching ideas, and building confidence in various entrepreneurial settings.

DAY 26

TECHNOLOGY TRENDS

SOW - See Page 171

KNOW - take 10 minutes today to read a book to help your leadership, growth, or knowledge

GROW - take 10 minutes to journal

SHOW - complete the challenge before you go to bed

TECHNOLOGY TRENDS

ACTION:
Stay updated on emerging technologies relevant to your industry.

Industry Research:
Explore recent technological advancements and trends within your industry. Make a list of technological advances that could help improve your business.

Tech News Consumption:
Dedicate time to regularly read technology news or follow industry blogs. The more tech news you can keep up-to-date on, then the more likely you will be to discover technology that can help your business.

Networking with Tech Professionals:
Connect with professionals in the technology sector to gain insights into emerging trends.

Application Brainstorming:
Consider how these technologies could be applied to enhance your business or industry.

Outcome:
Remaining informed on technology trends positions your business to adapt and innovate in a rapidly evolving landscape.

DAY 27

FINANCIAL PLANNING

SOW - See Page 173

KNOW - take 10 minutes today to read a book to help your leadership, growth, or knowledge

GROW - take 10 minutes to journal

SHOW - complete the challenge before you go to bed

FINANCIAL PLANNING

ACTION:
Refine your financial planning for sustainable business growth.

Financial Review:
Evaluate your current financial plan, considering revenue projections and expenses. Does your business have a plan to be profitable?

Adjustment Identification:
Identify areas where you can make adjustments to improve financial efficiency.

Emergency Fund Planning:
Plan to establish or enhance an emergency fund to mitigate unforeseen financial challenges. Do you have 3-6 months of business expenses set aside in the event an emergency happens?

Financial Advisor Consultation:
Consider seeking advice from a financial advisor to refine your financial strategies.

Outcome:
Continuous refinement of your financial plan ensures fiscal responsibility and resilience in the face of economic fluctuations. At the end of the day, how well you manage your resources will determine how successful and effective your business will be.

DAY

28

CELEBRATE!

SOW - See Page 175

KNOW - take 10 minutes today to read a book to help your leadership, growth, or knowledge

GROW - take 10 minutes to journal

SHOW - complete the challenge before you go to bed

CELEBRATE!

ACTION:
Acknowledge and celebrate your entrepreneurial achievements.

Achievement Reflection:
Reflect on the milestones and progress you've made in your entrepreneurial journey. Start making a list of those milestones and successes.

Gratitude Journaling:
Write down 3 things you are grateful for in relation to your business. What about things are motivating and inspiring?

Reward Yourself:
Treat yourself to a small reward or enjoyable activity as a celebration of your achievements. Even though you are self-employed, you still need recognition. So, reward yourself for the victories and successful moments.

Future Goals Setting:
Set new goals or milestones for the upcoming phase of your entrepreneurial journey.

Outcome:
Celebrating achievements reinforces motivation and provides a positive outlook as you continue to pursue your entrepreneurial dreams.

DAY

29

BUSINESS PLANNING

SOW - See Page 177

KNOW - take 10 minutes today to read a book to help your leadership, growth, or knowledge

GROW - take 10 minutes to journal

SHOW - complete the challenge before you go to bed

BUSINESS PLANNING

ACTION:
It's now time to polish and finalize your comprehensive business plan.

Review and Revise:
Review each section of your business plan, revising and updating as needed.

SWOT Analysis:
Conduct a final SWOT analysis to ensure your plan addresses strengths, weaknesses, opportunities, and threats.

Executive Summary Refinement:
Fine-tune your executive summary to provide a compelling overview of your business.

Peer Review:
Share your finalized business plan with a mentor or trusted advisor for feedback.

Outcome:
A well-crafted business plan serves as a roadmap for your entrepreneurial journey and is crucial for attracting investors and stakeholders.

DAY
30

COMMIT TO ACTION

SOW - See Page 179

KNOW - take 10 minutes today to read a book to help your leadership, growth, or knowledge

GROW - take 10 minutes to journal

SHOW - complete the challenge before you go to bed. Text your accountability mentor.

COMMIT TO ACTION

ACTION:
Make a commitment to take actionable steps toward your entrepreneurial dreams.

Letter to Yourself:
Write a letter to yourself, expressing your commitment to pursuing your entrepreneurial goals.

Action Plan:
Outline specific, achievable steps you will take in the next month to move closer to your business objectives.

Accountability Coach:
Share your commitments with a friend, family member, or mentor for support and accountability coaching.

Visualization:
Spend time visualizing yourself taking successful actions toward your goals.

Outcome:
This final day is about solidifying your commitment to the journey ahead and taking concrete steps towards realizing your entrepreneurial dreams.